THE DAILY LEARNER

BOOK 3

DAILY STOICISM

ALSO BY PARTH SAWHNEY

The Daily Apple

Thriving in the New Normal

The Way of the Karma Yogi

Elevation

The Detachment Manifesto

Becoming a Karma Yogi

DAILY STOICISM

---

21 Life-Changing Meditations on Philosophy and the Art of Living

PARTH SAWHNEY

Published by Parth Sawhney

DAILY STOICISM

First published in 2021

Contents

"And here lies the essential difference between Stoicism and the modern-day 'cult of optimism.' For the Stoics, the ideal state of mind was tranquility, not the excitable cheer that positive thinkers usually seem to mean when they use the word, 'happiness.' And tranquility was to be achieved not by strenuously chasing after enjoyable experiences, but by cultivating a kind of calm indifference towards one's circumstances."
— Oliver Burkeman

"A Stoic is someone who transforms fear into prudence, pain into transformation, mistakes into initiation, and desire into undertaking."
— Nassim Nicholas Taleb

"Being a Stoic does not mean being a robot. Being a Stoic means remaining calm both at the height of pleasure and the depths of misery."
— Abhijit Naskar

Introduction

I'm immensely grateful to you for choosing this book. This particular volume of *The Daily Learner* series is an attempt to distill the life-changing ideas from the best resources on Stoicism and philosophy in daily easy-to-read meditations.

Stoicism is a school of Hellenistic philosophy that was established by Zeno of Citium in the early 3rd century BC. It is a simple approach to overcome destructive emotions and act with reason.

The Stoic philosophy is predominantly about living ethically by practicing reason and logic. Also, it emphasizes living in accordance with nature. Later Stoic philosophers such as Seneca and Epictetus gave importance to cultivating virtues as they are sufficient to bring happiness to us and the people around us. The main premise was to shun all the moral corruption and be inspired to live like a Stoic Sage.

This philosophy has been practiced by both historical and modern men, including artists, kings, presidents, authors, and entrepreneurs. Stoicism provides useful tools and practical strategies to navigate through everyday problems and living a more meaningful and happy life.

If we want to transform our lives, then learning philosophy is not enough; we need to practice it as well. We can seek inspiration from Marcus Aurelius, the great Roman emperor, who reflected daily on the essential tenets of philosophy by writing personal notes to himself. In this way, he persuaded himself daily to stay on the right path by repeating to himself his observations and the lessons he learned touching the core tenets of the Stoic philosophy. As Tony Robbins has rightly said, "Repetition is the mother of skill"; we can change our core beliefs and enhance our mental skill set by repeating the important learnings every day to ourselves. John Maxwell echoes this truth in his book *The 15 Invaluable Laws of Growth* as well: "You will never change your life until you change something you do daily."

In the following pages, I have extracted the wisdom from the best resources on Stoicism and philosophy in a form that is easy to digest and consume (even if you're not a reader!). It's hard to capture an entire book in few words, but every mediation has been crafted to give you the essence and the formula, if you will, of the subject at hand or a groundbreaking idea introduced by the respective author or thought leader through his/her work. The repetition of the priceless gems and core tenets of Stoicism in these meditations is intentional in order to help you learn and internalize them in a quicker way. I'm sure the condensed timeless knowledge in these meditations will assist and guide you in navigating through the complexities that come with modern living. The fundamentals to attaining practical wisdom and living a good life will never change and that's why Stoicism has proven to be such an indispensable philosophy to learn the art of living.

Through this book, my intention for you is to develop a Stoic mindset over the next 21 days. Success is all about habits, and that's why I've chosen 21 days to get you started with the learning process. If you're serious about making a deep-level change in your psychology, I urge you to read the meditation once in the morning after you wake up, and once before sleeping at night. To make sure that this habit sticks, I would highly encourage you to keep reading or listening to books, podcasts, and other resources to continue your self-education in Stoicism.

As you read the meditations, some patterns will emerge. When internalized, they will guide you in your quest to living a virtuous and happy life. If any meditation piques your interest, feel free to embark further on your self-education journey and read the respective book. At the end of this book, I have gathered all the important takeaways and listed them in the final chapter, *Pithy Insights*, for your reference.

Once you are done reading this book, I would be grateful if you pay forward by recommending it to your loved ones. As you will learn in the following pages, cultivating a discipline to serve and contribute not only will help humanity but will add immense value, meaning, and purpose to your life as well.

Last but not the least, keep coming back to this book whenever you get a chance. As Robin Sharma has so eloquently put: "Education is inoculation to disruption. As you learn more, you can achieve more." I'll be honored if this book ends up becoming a part of your personal library and your quick go-to guide for re-calibrating to the Stoic mindset as you go ahead on your journey.

I hope you enjoy reading this book as much as I have enjoyed writing it.

Wishing you excellence and everlasting success!

Namaste and Efcharistó polý,

Parth Sawhney

Day 1: The Three Stoic Disciplines

"Control your perceptions. Direct your actions properly. Willingly accept what's outside your control."
— Ryan Holiday, *The Daily Stoic*

The foundation of Stoicism is built on three essential disciplines: The discipline of perception (how we see and perceive the world around us), the discipline of action (the decisions and actions we take - and to what end), and the discipline of will (how we deal with the things we cannot change, attain clear and convincing judgment, and come to a true understanding of our place in the world).

The Stoics tell us that by controlling our perceptions, we attain mental peace and clarity. By doing actions that are proper and just, we become more effective. And by cultivating will and acceptance, we find the power, wisdom, and strength to deal with anything the world throws at us. It was a belief that strengthening people in these three disciplines would help them cultivate resilience, grit, personal power, and profound joy in themselves.

Stoicism was born in a tumultuous ancient world where

everyday life was highly unpredictable. Hence, its primary aim was to provide effective and pragmatic tools that people could use to deal with daily life and thus ensure their well-being.

The Stoics believed that the most important human problems and issues faced by people whether they be of the past or in the future will remain the same as they were sure that both nature and human existence are never radically altered. Their mantra was: one day is as all days. And this has proved to be true even today as these disciplines have stood the test of time. It will be in our self-interest when we commit to them and abide by them as we live our lives.

Day 2: Logos

"The person who follows reason in all things will have both leisure and a readiness to act—they are at once both cheerful and self-composed."
— Marcus Aurelius, *Meditations*

The teachings of Marcus Aurelius and other ancient philosophers were built around the central aspect of *logos*. *Logos*, which roughly translates to reason, is considered as an essence that gives form and divine order to all the forms of life and the Universe. It reflects that all things happen for a reason.

Logos can be considered as an underlying master plan that orchestrates all the events that happen in this world, whether they are good or bad. We should have faith that all the things happening in our lives are happening for the best. The concept of *logos* encourages us to see a silver lining even when we are in the midst of chaos and storms of adversities.

Michael Singer asks a compelling question in his book *The Surrender Experiment*: "Am I better off making up an alternate reality in my mind and then fighting with reality to make it be my way, or am I better off letting go of what I want and serving the same forces of reality that managed to create the entire perfection of the Universe around me?" We need to have faith that everything is divinely orchestrated in our lives.

When we believe we are all a part of *logos* and we remain to be even after we die, our fear of death evaporates. If we look in the spiritual light, we are all eternal beings. To paraphrase Wayne Dyer, we are infinite spiritual beings having a temporary human experience. Like other things, even our death is planned by *logos* and can happen anytime. Hence, we need to live our lives in the best way we can and strive to become more productive and the best versions of ourselves. But also, we need to learn to let it go and become adaptable with regard to the events in our daily lives, meetings with people, and other activities that take away our time, as even these time taking and seemingly irrelevant activities are happening for a reason.

Since everything is being governed by *logos* and by reasoning and order, it makes sense for us to approach everything in our lives with a calm and analytical mind rather than being swept away by our emotions and feelings. Human emotions, especially negative ones, can be a serious threat to reason. So, in your daily life, if you feel stressed or overwhelmed, then the best strategy is to meditate on *logos* and the grand scheme of things.

We need to understand that both pain and suffering are a part of a bigger plan as well. When we complain about them, we disrespect and disregard the *logos* and that brings more pain and suffering to us. Instead, we should accept things the way they are and move on. When we trust *logos*, we get rid of all the fears: fears of death, pain, and suffering. We stop hating the work that we do for a living and resenting and questioning our place in society. Because we truly believe that everything is a part of a grander, flawless plan.

Day 3: Setting the Right Goals

"We should use our reasoning ability to overcome negative emotions. We should also use our reasoning ability to master our desires, to the extent that it is possible to do so. In particular, we should use reason to convince ourselves that things such as fame and fortune aren't worth having—not, at any rate, if what we seek is tranquility—and therefore aren't worth pursuing. Likewise, we should use our reasoning ability to convince ourselves that even though certain activities are pleasurable, engaging in those activities will disrupt our tranquility, and the tranquility lost will outweigh the pleasure gained."
— William B. Irvine, *A Guide to the Good Life*

It's worth investing our time, money, and energy in learning philosophy. The secret to living a good life, enriched with fulfillment is not to go to your dream school, get a prestigious degree and secure a high-paying job, but rather it is to learn the art of living through philosophy. Having a philosophy is analogous to having a roadmap; it helps us navigate through the ups and downs of life and find treasures that hold the deepest meaning to us.

Philosophy calls for introspection and defining goals that align with what we desire. This prevents us from having any regrets towards the end of our lives. In this world of constant distractions and countless ways where our attention is robbed from us, we can rely on Stoicism to help us in setting goals that align with us.

The path of Stoicism is that of moderation. It neither endorses a life of misery and poverty nor a life of luxury and hedonism. A Stoic enjoys the pleasures that life has to offer but he does not become dependent on them for his happiness. Stoicism teaches us that we should never rely on external objects for happiness as it is short-lived. Instead, we have to realize that the happiness and joy that we are seeking are always within us.

The Stoics had two primary goals: virtue and tranquility. They considered these as the foundational pillars for living a good life. Being virtuous is important because unlike animals and other beings we have the ability to reason and we must put it to good use. As our actions have the potential to affect the people around us, living a virtuous life not only helps us but also helps the people around us. Tranquility simply translates to eliminating all the negative emotions within us. In this way, we are in better charge of ourselves and don't let these negative emotions affect our decision-making ability and sabotage our success. We are able to gain clarity in difficult situations. The Stoics always believed that a mind that is calm and free of negativity can tackle any kind of obstacles that come up on the way.

Day 4: Converting Obstacles Into Opportunities

"The obstacle in the path becomes the path. Never forget, within every obstacle is an opportunity to improve our condition."
— Ryan Holiday, *The Obstacle Is the Way*

When things don't go our way and we face obstacles, we get angry and frustrated and that leads to experiencing a plethora of negative emotions. But if we change the lens through which we see obstacles, then we understand that these obstacles are in fact blessings that lead us to greater success. What stands in the way actually becomes the way.

Any obstacle can be converted into an advantage when we approach it through the eyes of a Stoic and focus on taking these three important steps:

1. *Perception*: We need to detach from the obstacle and look at it objectively. Instead of clouding your approach by taking things personally, imagine that you are giving advice to

a friend. We will never be able to turn our obstacles into an advantage unless we control our emotions. Preparing ourselves in advance for the worse case scenarios helps us remain calm when the circumstances are not in our favor and things don't go our way. Imagine how your mentor or a person of infinite wisdom would act. What approach would he or she take towards the obstacle? By changing the lens through which we see an obstacle, we start appreciating it and become aware of the hidden advantages that come with it. Sometimes it's all about looking at the larger context and knowing that the obstacle in itself is truly unimportant.

2. *Action*: Along with changing our perspective, we also need to focus on taking the right action. As we will continue facing obstacles in our lives, taking a single action every time is not enough. We need to cultivate a discipline of taking persistent action. As Napoleon Hill said, "The majority of people are ready to throw their aims and purposes overboard, and give up at the first sign of opposition or misfortune. A few carry on *despite* all opposition, until they attain their goal. These few are the Fords, Carnegies, Rockefellers, and Edisons. There may be no heroic connotation to the word persistence, but the quality is to the character of man what carbon is to steel." We need to keep taking action until we have overcome the obstacle. We need to come up with a plan of action and stick to it with incredible discipline. If you're faced with a massive problem, then we need to take a step-by-step approach and focus on taking small actions on a consistent basis. Through the *Compound Effect* and momentum, we can be certain that we will win over the obstacles. In

addition, once we understand that bigger obstacles also come with bigger weaknesses, we can learn how to turn obstacles against themselves.

3. *Will*: The most essential ingredient that can make all the difference in the world is your will. Unless you have unwavering faith in yourself and trust your capabilities, you will have a hard time overcoming obstacles. Will is what guides us in our perceptions and actions. The ancient Stoic philosophers exercised their will by focusing on the question: *What things are in my control and what are not?* We have little ability to control external factors and the environment around us but what we do have control over is our internal state and the emotions that we are experiencing. As we face and overcome these internal obstacles, we get in a better position to face and overcome the external ones as well. A disciplined will gives us the power to face the most difficult obstacles head-on. Through a focused will, we don't let our personal situation and current circumstances discourage us from pursuing the most important goals in our life. We are able to unlock our true potential and break through the barriers of human possibility.

Day 5: Practicing Philosophy

"My advice is really this: what we hear the philosophers saying and what we find in their writings should be applied in our pursuit of the happy life. We should hunt out the helpful pieces of teaching, and the spirited and noble-minded sayings which are capable of immediate practical application—not far-fetched or archaic expressions or extravagant metaphors and figures of speech—and learn them so well that words become works. No one to my mind lets humanity down quite so much as those who study philosophy as if it were a sort of commercial skill and then proceed to live in a quite different manner from the way they tell other people to live."

— Seneca, *Letters from a Stoic*

A true Stoic is someone who is committed and dedicated to cultivating a self-reliant mindset, mastering philosophy, and achieving long-lasting happiness. We all need philosophy to bring order and purpose to our lives. Through philosophy, we can mold our personality so that it supports our best interests. We become disciplined, focused, and participate in actions that add value to our lives as well as others'. It's like a compass that guides us and helps us in correcting our course when we get caught up in storms and lose sight of our destination. Without philosophy, we will never be able to detach from the anxieties and worries that emerge in us.

Countless situations may arise in our daily lives where we may feel lost and need advice. In those cases, we can look up to philosophy and cultivate wisdom so that we make better decisions. Not only does philosophy help us in overcoming obstacles but it also helps us in the process of healing. Philosophy soothes us when we are feeling down. As Marcus Aurelius reminded himself in one of his reflections: "And not to think of philosophy as your instructor, but as the sponge and egg white that relieve ophthalmia—as a soothing ointment, a warm lotion."

There are some people who spend a great amount of time learning philosophy, but they never put it into action. Philosophy is meant for education and implementation, not for entertainment. One important teaching mentioned in the book *The Law of Attraction: The Basics of the Teachings of Abraham* by Esther Hicks is that: "Words do not teach, and only life experience teaches, but the combination of life experience coupled with words that define and explain can enhance the experience of learning." Philosophy can be your manual for life but only when you engage in action. And it loses its purpose when you don't put it into practice.

Seneca teaches us that happiness cannot be attained by something external and materialistic but rather it can be experienced through the practice of philosophy. Let go of all the distractions and temptations and dedicate your time and energy to the study and practice of philosophy. Become a person of substance and integrity towards yourself and others; a person who is calm, intellectual, and giving, and an ideal for society.

Day 6: The Pursuit of a Good Life

"Demand not that things happen as you wish, but wish them to happen as they do, and you will go on well."

— Epictetus, *The Discourses*

For Epictetus, the primary goal of philosophy was living a good life rather than understanding the world and that started with attaining inner tranquility. Embracing this tranquility within meant conforming to nature, appreciating and accepting *logos,* and living by the truth.

Epictetus observed that there are three stages that we humans need to go through in order to achieve a good life.

1. *Mastery of Desires*: We often think happiness is conditional and is based on the fulfillment of our desires. Our happiness is tied to other people and their behaviors and when they don't respond to us in the way we expect them to, we end up disappointed and sad. The philosophers teach us that if we base our happiness on others' actions and reactions, we end up living a life of envy, anger, and re-

sentment. Instead of setting unrealistic expectations from other people, we need to make sure that our expectations and judgments are reasonable. We need to make sure that our desires are in the realm of our power. Our wants and desires can be controlled by us but what we cannot control is how other people and the world responds to us. We can only control the internal and hence should let go of the external.

2. *Duties*: We need to understand that a person is not an individual entity detached from the world, but he/she is an important contributor to it. We are the world and the world is us. Stoic philosophers referred to human beings as citizens of the world, and unlike other living beings, we have duties to perform. We have the capability to discern the purpose behind the divine orchestration of events and connect the dots. It's a prerogative for us human beings to understand "the connection of things" and hence it's our duty to live a life that aligns with this truth. Our duties are measured by our relationships and it's our responsibility to engage in pursuits that align with our core essence and nature and avoid the ones that sway us from our path.

3. *Right thinking*: The third stage consists of cultivating the discipline of logic and disputation. Having the right way of thinking is essential to understand a person's duty towards his/her creator and peers. To make sure that our actions don't affect us and the people around us, we need to be logical and commit to learning how we can avoid deception and manipulation. We should stay away from making rash and hasty decisions that may have negative consequences. With the right thinking and perspective, we can see things in the right light and appreciate their

positive aspects rather than focusing on the negative ones. Being logical and having the right mindset can be a lifesaver in difficult situations.

16

Day 7: Freedom Leads to Happiness

"People are not disturbed by things, but by the views they take of them."

"If you ever happen to turn your attention to externals, for the pleasure of any one, be assured that you have ruined your scheme of life. Be contented, then, in everything, with being a philosopher; and if you with to seem so likewise to any one, appear so to yourself, and it will suffice you."

— Epictetus, *Enchiridion*

Being free is an essential component of being happy. The power of reason can be liberating as it helps us in focusing on the aspect of lives that we have control over and letting go of those that we cannot control. We have control over our attitude, choices, and behaviors, and that's what we should exercise. Trying to control external circumstances such as other people and their behaviors, stock market, and material possessions will never work out in our favor.

We have little to no control over certain situations such as death, natural calamities, and sickness, and instead of fighting against it, we should surrender and let it go. We don't have control over them and we only have control over our thoughts, actions, and reactions. True happiness can only be secured when you let go of the frustrating pursuit of things that we have no control over. Thich Nhat Hanh in his book *The Heart of the Buddha's Teaching* writes, "Letting go gives us freedom, and freedom is the only condition for happiness. If, in our heart, we still cling to anything - anger, anxiety, or possessions - we cannot be free." Whether it be our favorite cup getting chipped or some event as difficult as a loved one dying, reason reminds us of the ephemeral nature of things around us and the mortality of our human life. We, humans, try to avoid situations and people that cause us pain and despair, but reason reveals to us that it's not those things but our perception of those things that dictates the state of affairs. Hence, to reach a state of happiness, an important step that we can take is correcting our will, perception, and accepting things as they are.

Epictetus through his philosophy teaches us that controlling our desires and aversions is the key to living a happy life. When we let go of our judgments towards external circumstances and shift our perspectives to accepting things as they are and controlling our responses towards them, we experience true freedom and happiness.

Day 8: The Four Cardinal Virtues

"One of the first lessons from Stoicism, then, is to focus our attention and efforts where we have the most power and then let the universe run as it will. This will save us both a lot of energy and a lot of worry."
— Massimo Pigliucci, *How to Be a Stoic*

To become a Stoic, we need to practice virtue and excellence in our lives and let them be our guide in the roller coaster journey of life. We need to be mindful of all the consequences of our actions, not only on others but primarily on ourselves. Stoicism is not only about learning how to take the right actions but also about how we can tap into the correct moral and psychological dimension before we act.

Virtues not only help us in identifying obstacles but also help us in staying grounded and calm. Below are the four cardinal virtues of Stoicism:

1. **Practical Wisdom**: Overcoming obstacles and complex situations in the best way possible with the resources

available in hand.

2. **Courage**: To not be swayed by desires and pleasures, and do what is right in all circumstances. To do righteous actions both physically and morally.

3. **Justice**: To treat every individual as equal with fairness and kindness regardless of their financial and social status, caste, color, creed, or ethnicity.

4. **Temperance**: To exercise moderation and self-control in all aspects of life.

Day 9: The Dichotomy of Control

"However, the majority of people mistakenly judge external things to be 'good' and therefore experience feelings of desire for things beyond their control, leading to frustration and suffering."
— Donald Robertson, *Stoicism and the Art of Happiness*

The Stoics advise us to distinguish between things that we can control and things that we cannot. We should let go and accept the things that are not under our control and focus on doing actions and the variables that we can control.

When we act virtuously with the best information that we have, using the best tools and resources, and giving our best, then we have done our job and we should not have any other concerns lingering in our minds. The outcomes of those actions are not in our control. Think of favorable outcomes as a cherry on top of the cake.

When we perform inspired actions that are meaningful and when they are done from a place of alignment, we are on the right track to success. Sometimes this may involve suffering but because our actions are meaningful to us, we end up attracting happiness in the long run. The subtle art of happiness involves alignment with our actions and not with our results. When we act with the virtues of Stoicism and embrace the tranquility inside us even if there are disturbances, obstacles, or chaos around us, we become the beacon of hope and happiness. Happiness is always within and we have access to it anytime. And if we want to make others happy, we need to generate happiness within ourselves first. Learning the art to be happy is one of the most selfless acts you can do. As Gretchen Rubin remarked in her book *The Happiness Project*, "The belief that unhappiness is selfless and happiness is selfish is misguided. It's more selfless to act happy."

Both acceptance and letting go of the circumstances around us can make us happy. In the midst of dark times, when you cultivate the light of happiness within you and share it with other people, brightness follows soon.

Day 10: Becoming a Lifelong Learner

"Ego is the enemy of what you want and of what you have: Of mastering a craft. Of real creative insight. Of working well with others. Of building loyalty and support. Of longevity. Of repeating and retaining your success. It repulses advantages and opportunities. It's a magnet for enemies and errors. It is Scylla and Charybdis."
— Ryan Holiday, *Ego Is the Enemy*

Epictetus remarked that it is impossible for a man to learn what he thinks he already knows. If we think that we are experts in our craft or our field of interest, we become susceptible to getting influenced by our egos. Instead of considering ourselves as a know-it-all, it's much better to humble ourselves. We should always consider ourselves as a learner — someone who's improving every day in his or her craft. In that way, we are always striving for growth and feeding our grit. Even if you are incredibly good at something, you can tame down your ego by accepting that there is someone in this world who is even better than you.

As the popular story goes, a man once went to a wise Zen Master to seek wisdom and learn about attaining enlightenment. The Master welcomed him and offered to discuss this over tea. As the tea was served, the Zen Master kept pouring tea even after the cup was filled. As the tea kept overflowing, the visitor could not restrain him any longer and asked him to stop pouring as there was no room for more tea. The Master smiled and offered his gem of wisdom: "Like this cup of tea, you are full of your own opinions and speculations as well. How can I teach you unless you empty your cup?" This story is a great reminder for us that in order to learn something new, we need to unlearn all the previous knowledge with regard to that subject first. We need to start with a fresh pair of eyes and a beginner's mind. There's a wise quote by Shunryu Suzuki-roshi: "In the beginner's mind there are many possibilities, in the expert's there are few."

When we work with other immensely talented people, our ego remains in check. We should always be open to learning new things and improving our craft. Something that stops us from improving our work and feeds our ego is pride. Pride and ego are great friends, but our worst enemies. The shortcomings of pride are that we stop learning and challenging and pushing our limits; we become overly sensitive to criticism. To become a perennial performer, we need to let go of our pride and ego and not let them affect our success.

Day 11: Life Can Be Long

"It is not that we have so little time but that we lose so much. The life we receive is not short but we make it so; we are not ill provided but use what we have wastefully."
— Seneca, *On the Shortness of Life*

We get so busy with trivialities and instant gratifications that we lose the essence of living. We get caught up in achieving our goals and think that once we achieve them we'll be happy, but this hardly happens. We get into all kinds of materialistic pursuits thinking success means getting stuff. Life seems short and unfulfilled. Our goal should be a life of meaning and purpose, not one inclined to pursuing luxuries.

To live an extraordinary life, we need to commit to self-education and self-improvement. We need mentors and coaches to guide us in the right direction. We can seek guidance and wisdom from philosophers, thinkers, and successful people through the books they have written. Through self-education, we'll be on our path to positivity, prosperity, and success. This prolongs our life and enhances its quality.

We have to identify our interests and only engage in work that makes us happy and fulfilled. And to use our strengths for the betterment of mankind through our work. Along with work, we also have to give importance to having fun. Overexertion will diminish our enthusiasm. There is no harm in indulging in pleasures. A healthy balance is what we should strive for.

Day 12: Strengthening Our Inner Fortress

"Objectivity is a virtue and one that is very difficult to practice."
"Do what you must; let happen what may."
— Pierre Hadot, *The Inner Citadel*

If we want to transform our lives, then learning philosophy is not enough; we need to practice it as well. Only then we will be able to learn effectively from our life experiences. Marcus Aurelius realized this truth. He reflected daily on the essential tenets of philosophy by writing personal notes to himself (*hypomnemata*). This was a way for him to use the voice of philosophy to strengthen himself and his personal voice. He wrote them for himself so that he could be in a better place psychologically and spiritually. In this way, he persuaded himself daily to stay on the right path by repeating to himself his observations and the lessons he learned touching the core tenets of the Stoic philosophy. As Tony Robbins rightly said, "Repetition is the mother of skill," this was the way for him to strengthen his core beliefs and mental skill set by repeating the important learnings every day to himself.

We can say that these meditations are akin to spiritual exercises for self-discovery and self-transformation. Through writing these meditations, Marcus Aurelius was following the teachings of Epictetus of writing the fundamental principles of the Stoic philosophy every day. Through close observation of his meditations, we can distill down three dogmas that can help us in navigating pragmatically in our own experiences without losing our calm. These dogmas are: being content with whatever happens, being just and accepting of others, and being able to apply rules of discernment to our own inner representations of external circumstances. These dogmas correspond well with the three disciplines of Stoic philosophy: *perception*, *action*, and *will*. When we live by these three dogmas and cultivate the three disciplines, we strengthen our inner fortress and develop the inner attitudes of acceptance to the divine orchestration, justice, serving others, and detachment by being objective.

Marcus Aurelius engaged in the spiritual exercises of writing meditations every day so that he could bring these dogmas to life and internalize and live by them. And we can do the same for ourselves by dedicating some time every day to reflect on our life experiences and bridge the gap between philosophy and its practice by writing down our essential realizations and the lessons we learn from philosophy and life. In that way, we'll be able to live the philosophy pragmatically and enjoy and accept life as it unfolds. By doing these spiritual exercises, we get a chance to be in tune with our emotions, our core values, our awareness, our intuition, and our moral compass. We are able to zoom out and look at the bigger picture, and hence work on building a better vision not only for ourselves and our lives, but for the world and for the entire humanity.

29

Day 13: Focusing on the Right Things

"There is a time and place for diversion and amusements, but you should never allow them to override your true purposes."

"Some things are in our control and others not. Things in our control are opinion, pursuit, desire, aversion, and, in a word, whatever are our own actions. Things not in our control are body, property, reputation, command, and, in one word, whatever are not our own actions."

— Epictetus, *The Art of Living*

Epictetus guided himself and his life by asking two essential questions:

1. *How do I live a happy and fulfilling life?*
2. *How can I be a good person?*

This single-minded passion is reflected in his teachings is as well; a strong point of Epictetus' philosophy is focusing on ourselves and our actions. Marcus Aurelius, who was also one of the people that benefited from his lectures, echoed this notion in his reflections when he wrote about what he learned from Epictetus: "to put up with discomfort... Have no time for slanderers."

Epictetus always focused on living a good life. For him, a happy life and a virtuous life, where we focus on the right things for ourselves and others, were synonymous. Epictetus teaches us that happiness and personal fulfillment are the byproducts of doing the right thing. Not all events that happen in our lives are in our control and we need to cultivate acceptance towards fate and life as it happens. Epictetus' teachings can be summed up into three core ideas: knowing what we can control and mastering our desires, performing our duties and doing the right actions, and learning to think clearly about ourselves, our relationships, and our role within the larger community of humanity.

Day 14: Modern Practices, Ancient Roots

"Epictetus compares the mind to a bottle of water with a ray of light shining through it, representing our perception of external events. If the water is shaken, the light is refracted and disturbed. Likewise, when our mind, judgements, and perceptions are internally disturbed, external events look disturbing to us. We project our feelings on to external events."

— Donald Robertson, *The Philosophy of Cognitive-Behavioural Therapy (CBT)*

The origins of modern Cognitive-Behavioral Therapy (CBT) can be traced back to the therapeutic practices in the ancient era of Stoicism. A clear analogy can be observed between ancient philosophy and modern CBT as there are various concepts and techniques that overlap between the two.

The quote by Epictetus: "What upsets people is not things themselves but their judgments about the things," is commonly referred to within the literature on CBT, as it addresses the fundamental framework of CBT which is understanding the relationship between cognition and emotion. It is a common misconception that Stoicism is an intellectualized philosophical approach that doesn't count emotional responses. In reality, it encourages us to cultivate an attitude of indifference towards things and events that we don't have control over so that we can avoid unnecessary emotional discomfort and pain. The Stoics saw emotional suffering as a consequence of giving more importance to these things and events than they really deserved along with errors in logic and reasoning. Stoicism not only accommodates emotions but also encourages cultivating a rational love towards humanity and existence as a whole.

The daily practice of recalling and writing the essential tenets and dogmas of the philosophy align well with the modern practice of autosuggestion, affirmations, journaling, and the use of coping statements in CBT. Also, the adoption of mindfulness meditation in modern CBT has deeper roots in Stoicism where developing mindfulness towards our own faculty of thinking and the internal dialogue, focusing on cultivating clarity in our thoughts and actions, and embracing the present moment was encouraged.

In addition to the fact that there are parallels between Stoicism and modern psychotherapy, we also need to understand that learning philosophy helps us to look at the bigger picture and hence it plays an important role within the overarching context of 'the art of living.'

Day 15: The Captain of My Soul

"So what Epictetus was telling his students was that there can be no such thing as being the 'victim' of another. You can only be a 'victim of yourself.' It's all in how you discipline your mind."
— James B. Stockdale, *Courage Under Fire*

James Bond Stockdale, one of the American prisoners of war in Vietnam, endured unimaginable torture and brutality. He lived for years enduring intense pain, both physical and emotional. His only solace was the teachings of Epictetus that stopped him from being broken and envision a life of sanity again. In those dark years, in spite of the various attempts of the interrogators to generate shame, fear, and guilt, Stockdale had only one focus: to control his emotions and not give in to them.

Our emotions are our own and we have absolute voluntary control over them. And if we face situations where we don't have any control, we have to adapt. We cannot take responsibility for what happens around us, but we can cast around us an invisible shield so that we protect our emotions.

If we give up control over our emotions, we become powerless and that's when we experience a true defeat. Stockdale made a valid point that the notions of good and evil only exist within our hearts and what gives them meaning is within our will and our power. As the last verse of Ernest Henley's poem *Invictus* goes:

> It matters not how strait the gate,
> How charged with punishment the scroll,
> I am the master of my fate:
> I am the captain of my soul.

Day 16: Antifragility

"Difficulty is what wakes up the genius."
— Nassim Nicholas Taleb, *Antifragile*

We have all come across packages with the label 'Fragile - Handle with care.' This warning, of course, means that if subjected to stress or carelessness the contents inside would break.

According to the Merriam-Webster dictionary, fragile is

1. easily broken or destroyed
2. constitutionally delicate: lacking in vigor

When subjected to volatile situations, fragile things break. But there are times when volatility ends up benefiting the object instead of degrading it. The concept of antifragility applies to things that benefit from harm caused by volatile and adverse circumstances. Unlike fragile things that break under stress, antifragile things gain an advantage and become better.

A couple of good examples are coal undergoing immense heat and pressure over time to become a priceless piece of diamond, and the rock or a piece of marble that has to go to countless blows of the chisel, till it becomes a beautiful piece of art.

Antifragility is fueled by unity. Even if the individual components may be fragile, when they get together, they can build a system that can be highly antifragile in nature. For instance, people or businesses themselves can be considered fragile on their own, but when they work harmoniously in a system, they become unbeatable. When faced with misfortune or a natural calamity, people tend to unite and hence gain strength.

We can train both our body and mind to be antifragile. The quality of an antifragile system is that it not only strengthens you when you face stresses or shockers but also prepares you for any future possible adversities. This happens by the principle of overcompensation, which is the hallmark of antifragility: Strength develops by overcompensating against adversities.

Antifragility may give you an added physical and mental strength, which you may not need right now. Hence, the time and energy that you spend on cultivating the strength may seem futile and lacking intention. But if a situation demands in future where you are subjected to use it, whether it be carrying a huge piece of furniture when you move or facing a big obstacle in your business where you need to come up with a quick and effective solution, all these efforts to become antifragile pay off.

If you want to achieve and maintain extraordinary success in this ever-changing and unpredictable world then antifragility is the most useful skill that you can develop. The antifragility that develops from the chaos around us actually helps us in preparing ourselves so that the next time the same situation or circumstances arise we are better equipped and ready to face them. In this way, antifragility can act as a very valuable instrument in converting chaos to order and making us stronger and wiser in the process.

Day 17: Controlling Our Emotions

"The founders of the Stoic school did not set out to suppress or deny our natural feelings; rather, it was their endeavor, in psychology as in ethics, to determine what the natural feelings of humans really are. With the emotions we most often experience they were certainly dissatisfied; their aim, however, was not to eliminate feelings as such from human life, but to understand what sort of affective responses a person would have who was free of false belief."
— Margaret R. Graver, *Stoicism and Emotion*

We think our emotions drive us because we feel that they are largely involuntary and we have no control over them. Our emotional impulses sometimes work in our favor and sometimes we end up doing actions that we regret later on. The Stoics explain that there are different causes of our emotions and some of them include our misaligned beliefs. According to Chrysippus, emotions are nothing but judgments that involve beliefs about value.

When we face a situation that is not favorable or if we get

results that are not in concurrence with our beliefs and desires, we become susceptible to our emotions. If we don't keep a check on them, feelings of anger, envy, jealousy, or resentment may emerge within us as a consequence. Beliefs are patterns that we have cultivated over time and because these emotions are driven by our beliefs, we are responsible for these emotions. Our beliefs have contributed to the development of our character and the traits that we have gathered over time, whether good or bad. Hence, it'll be wise for us to run a diagnostic check of our core values and beliefs.

We can start with a blank slate and get rid of all the beliefs that don't serve us. By taking back control of the deep-seated beliefs inside us and changing them, we are in better control of the emotions that we experience. As we gently guide us towards experiencing positive emotions, life becomes easier and effortless for us. Esther Hicks in her book, *The Astonishing Power of Emotions*, beautifully writes about the role of emotions in our well-being: "When you feel love or joy—or any positive emotion—you are literally being the expanded version that life has caused you to become. When you feel fear, anger, or despair—or any negative emotion—you are not, in this moment, by virtue of whatever it is that you are giving your attention to, allowing yourself to be that new expanded version … you are not letting yourself keep up with who you have become."

Day 18: Philosophy Is for Life

"Take our new philosophical insights and repeat them until they become new automatic habits. Philosophy is not merely a process of abstract reflection, but a practice. 'We acquire the virtues by practice,' Aristotle wrote."

— Jules Evans, *Philosophy for Life and Other Dangerous Situations*

Even though there are similarities between ancient philosophy and modern therapies such as CBT, there are some stark differences as well. While CBT or a coaching session focuses on a short-term fix, adopting ancient philosophy is a lifestyle: a life-long discipline to be cultivated and practiced every day.

CBT lasts for a few weeks or months, but in ancient times it was advised to study philosophy every day to internalize wisdom and always be prepared to face challenges that life threw at us. Philosophy not only helps us in managing mental disorders but also helps in navigating through life as it is a recurrent therapy for the soul. Philosophy is not about prescription — it's a lifestyle and requires a renewed commitment every day. To echo the thoughts of the ancient philosophers, simple goals of reading self-help books, taking an online personal development course, participating in a session with a therapist or a life coach, and doing techniques such as goal setting are not enough. These approaches are more individualistic and what we need is a change in our perspective so that we can zoom out and look at the bigger picture. That may mean contemplating over the meaning of life, our existence, the Universe as a whole, and what roles we play in it.

The Stoics placed huge importance on being in harmony with the Universe and the way it works. They firmly believed in the rational intelligence that permeates everything. Hence, in order to live a happy and peaceful life, they believed it was their duty to act rationally with reason and logic so that they can be better aligned with the Universe. The discipline of philosophy keeps us deep-rooted into this truth.

The Stoics believed in the preparation of body and mind on a daily basis so that we are better equipped to face hardships, whether big or small. By training ourselves with the virtues of inner fortitude, acceptance, and committing to the study and implementation of philosophy every day, we ensure that we live a life that is good in all ways, a life that is in alignment with our inner truths.

Day 19: Ask Better Questions

"...What is remarkable about the Greeks—even pre-philosophically—is that despite the salience of religious rituals in their lives, when it came to the question of what it is that makes an individual human life worth living they didn't look to the immortals but rather approached the question in mortal terms. Their approaching the question of human mattering in human terms is the singularity that creates the conditions for philosophy in ancient Greece, most especially as these conditions were realized in the city-state of Athens."
— Rebecca Goldstein, *Plato at the Googleplex*

Times have changed drastically but we can still go back to the ancient Stoic philosophy to understand ourselves better and be able to live a much more happy and meaningful life. Plato's teachings can be an indispensable tool to understand how our minds work and how we can elevate our lives and bring purpose and meaning to our existence. If we can take away one important lesson from his philosophy, it is that we should ask questions. As the wise quote by Socrates goes: "The unexamined life is not worth living."

In our daily lives, we simply accept the way society works. But we never question why things are the way they are and what are the values on which it is built. Instead, we should cultivate a curious and inquisitive mindset and question everything. Unless we do that, we won't be able to change things and either make them better or come up with better solutions. Plato explained that the foundation of living an extraordinary life is to improve our reasoning consistently and questioning and contemplating the beliefs that we have harbored and accepted. To paraphrase Dr. John Demartini, the quality of your life is determined by the quality of the questions that you ask.

In today's technologically advanced times, if we have a question in our mind, the first place that we go to is Google. With an enhanced search engine, we can find answers to our daily problems instantly. But when it comes to the questions regarding moral and ethical dilemmas, Google is not a useful tool. During those hard times, we can turn to philosophy to seek guidance and direction. Instead of relying on search engines, algorithms, and technology, we can focus our attention on learning from the rhythms of nature and life.

When we get on the trail of asking deeper questions about life, humanity, meaning, and purpose, we start creating a life that is not only happy and fulfilling but extraordinary in every aspect.

Day 20: Stoicism in the Modern Era

"Stoic ethics is a species of eudaimonism. Its central, organizing concern is about what we ought to do or be to live well—to flourish. That is, we make it a lemma that all people ought to pursue a good life for themselves as a categorical commitment second to none. It does not follow from this that they ought to pursue any one particular version of the good life, or to cling tenaciously to the one they are pursuing.

Living virtuously is the process of creating a single, spatiotemporal object—a life. A life has a value as an object, as a whole. It is not always the case that its value as an object will be a function of the value of its spatiotemporal parts considered separately. But it is always the case that an evaluation of the parts will be incomplete until they are understood in the context of the whole life. What seems so clearly valuable (or required or excellent) when we focus on a thin temporal slice of a life (or a single, long strand of a life) may turn out to be awful or optional or vicious when we take a larger view. And it is the life as a whole that we consider when we think about its value

in relation to other things, or its value as a part of the cosmos."
— Lawrence C. Becker, *A New Stoicism*

Times have changed and it may be a challenge for us to figure out how we can fit Stoicism and the teachings of various philosophers in our modern lifestyle. As the nature of the Universe and the nature of humanity have not changed, most of the fundamental thoughts remain the same. The magical doctrines mentioned in the ancient scriptures can still guide us when we are faced with obstacles and dilemmas.

We definitely need to have a new approach and bring into the picture the advancement of technology, science, medicine, and the way we interact with other people. Philosophy can be a wonderful antidote and soothe us whenever we encounter fading humanity. Not only it helps us in getting grounded again, but it also reminds us of the truths that have stood the test of time.

There are some brilliant takeaways from the ancient Stoic philosophy that can add the depth that we need in our fast-paced lives. The teachings of ethics and relying on practical tools and strategies rather than moral theory are indispensable in today's society. The way we experience life has changed immensely, however, the basic approach that we should cultivate towards obstacles and daily challenges remain the same and that's where Stoicism can come to our rescue.

The philosophy of intentionalism and logic transfer very well in today's times where we are constantly bombarded with distractions and are fighting the urge to collect material possessions. It's hard to find the voice of our inner being in the noise that surrounds us. We are always busy or pretending to be busy however we lack productivity, focus, and the burning desire within us to finish what we started. The movement of reductive materialism or minimalism can be a lifesaver and has parallels with the Stoic philosophy. Decluttering our spaces and our minds can start churning the engines of a meaningful life and bringing more purpose and clarity to us.

Last but not the least, the emotional roller coaster that we get on in our daily lives, further enhanced by media, can wreak havoc in our lives if we don't pay close attention to it. The Stoics discouraged getting into unwanted and irrelevant emotional trains of thought caused by misunderstandings and inappropriate reactions. Instead, they encouraged cultivating *eupatheiai* or "good emotional states". We have the power to generate happiness within us and remain untouchable by the chaos around us. Through Stoic philosophy, we can embrace and enjoy the inner calm within us. The detachment towards circumstances and obstacles not only protects us but also assists us in finding solutions and resolving issues. Becoming emotionally intelligent and strong not only helps us, but it is of immense value to the people that surround us and the ones we love.

Day 21: Changing Our Beliefs

"Sometimes the features most worth preserving are exactly the broad outlines, the structural and architectonic connections between parts... In studying Stoicism, we can find all sorts of small phrases and images that are attractive and easily taken away. But we can also learn from the interconnectedness of the whole system, even when we can no longer support or embrace the system as a whole."
— Tad Brennan, *The Stoic Life*

We human beings are rational creatures. Our ethical judgments are initiated by 'impressions,' which are basically the perceptions that we harbor towards objects around us. Unlike animals that respond automatically to these impressions, we tend to assess them. And that takes us to one of the following decisions:

1. We think our impression is accurate based on the data we have collected over time and say *'yes'* to it, or
2. We don't hold our impression to be correct; we may or

may not need to collect more data to reach a conclusion, but for now, we say *'no'* to it.

The aforementioned *'yes'* is called an 'assent' (*sunkatathesis*). Based on our assents to impressions, we form beliefs in our minds. These beliefs dictate how we see the world and our opinions towards things objects and events; these may be true or false. As we grow up and live in our society, we are influenced continuously by its common beliefs. Unfortunately, some of these beliefs are not true and we end up cultivating a herd mentality. We end up living mediocre lives because our beliefs and expectations are defined by the people around us. Advertisements and constant bombardment by media make us believe in false truths and we end up navigating our lives in the wrong direction. There's a chance that our perceptions of health, wealth, and living a successful life, defined by society and others, maybe completely incorrect. Unfortunately, these false beliefs set up the operating system for us based on which we take intentional misguided actions. These actions have the potential of sabotaging our well-being, finances, reputation, and our long-term success and fulfillment.

A core concept in Stoic moral psychology is that of rational impulse or *hormê*. These impulses are basically psychological events that are defined by our set of beliefs and they eventually manifest into actions. Hence, our success and happiness are much dictated by our internal belief system. In order to live an extraordinary life and fight mediocrity, it is crucial that we first decimate all of our limiting beliefs. As Vironika Tugaleva beautifully said, "Courage is your natural setting. You do not need to become courageous, but rather peel back the layers of self-protective, limiting beliefs that keep you small."

Pithy Insights

- *The foundation of Stoicism is built on three essential disciplines: The discipline of perception (how we see and perceive the world around us), the discipline of action (the decisions and actions we take - and to what end), and the discipline of will (how we deal with the things we cannot change, attain clear and convincing judgment, and come to a true understanding of our place in the world).*

- *The teachings of Marcus Aurelius and other ancient philosophers were built around the central aspect of logos. Logos can be considered as an underlying master plan that orchestrates all the events that happen in this world, whether they are good or bad. We should have faith that all the things happening in our lives are happening for the best.*

- *When we complain, we disrespect and disregard the logos and that brings more pain and suffering to us. Instead, we should accept things the way they are and move on.*

- *The secret to living a good life, enriched with fulfillment is to learn the art of living through philosophy. Having a philosophy is analogous to having a road map; it helps us navigate through the ups and downs of life and find treasures that hold the deepest meaning to us.*

- *The path of Stoicism is that of moderation. It neither endorses a life of misery and poverty nor a life of luxury and hedonism.*

- *The Stoics had two primary goals: virtue and tranquility. They considered these as the foundational pillars for living a good life.*
- *The Stoics always believed that a mind that is calm and free of negativity can tackle any kind of obstacles that come up on the way.*
- *Any obstacle can be converted into an advantage when we approach it through the eyes of a Stoic.*
- *We need to detach from the obstacle and look at it objectively. We will never be able to turn obstacles into opportunities unless we control our emotions. By changing the lens through which we see an obstacle, we start appreciating it and become aware of the hidden advantages that come with it.*
- *Preparing ourselves in advance for the worse case scenarios helps us remain calm when the circumstances are not in our favor and things don't go our way.*
- *Once we understand that bigger obstacles also come with bigger weaknesses, we can learn how to turn obstacles against themselves.*
- *The most essential ingredient that can make all the difference in the world is your will. Unless you have unwavering faith in yourself and trust your capabilities, you will have a hard time overcoming obstacles.*
- *The ancient Stoic philosophers exercised their will by focusing on the question: What things are in my control and what are not?*
- *Through a focused will, we are able to unlock our true potential and break through the barriers of human possibility.*
- *A true Stoic is someone who is committed and dedicated to cultivating a self-reliant mindset, mastering philosophy, and achieving long-lasting happiness.*

- *Countless situations may arise in our daily lives where we may feel lost and need advice. In those cases, we can look up to philosophy and cultivate wisdom so that we make better decisions.*
- *Philosophy is meant for education and implementation, not for entertainment.*
- *Instead of setting unrealistic expectations from other people, we need to make sure that our expectations and judgments are reasonable. We need to make sure that our desires are in the realm of our power.*
- *Stoic philosophers referred to human beings as citizens of the world, and unlike other living beings, we have duties to perform. We have the capability to discern the purpose behind the divine orchestration of events and connect the dots.*
- *It's a prerogative for us human beings to understand "the connection of things" and hence it's our duty to live a life that aligns with this truth.*
- *With the right thinking and perspective, we can see things in the right light and appreciate their positive aspects rather than focusing on the negative ones. Being logical and having the right mindset can be a lifesaver in difficult situations.*
- *True happiness can only be secured when you let go of the frustrating pursuit of things that we have no control over.*
- *To become a Stoic, we need to practice virtue and excellence in our lives and let them be our guide in the roller coaster journey of life.*
- *Stoicism is not only about learning how to take the right actions but also about how we can tap into the correct moral and psychological dimension before we act.*
- *The four cardinal virtues of Stoicism are:*

1. *Practical Wisdom*
2. *Courage*
3. *Justice*
4. *Temperance*

- *The Stoics advise us to distinguish between things that we can control and things that we cannot. We should let go and accept the things that are not under our control and focus on doing actions and the variables that we can control.*
- *When we act with the virtues of Stoicism and embrace the tranquility inside us even if there are disturbances, obstacles, or chaos around us, we become the beacon of hope and happiness.*
- *Instead of considering ourselves as a know-it-all, it's much better to humble ourselves. We should always consider ourselves as a learner; someone who's improving every day in his or her craft.*
- *To become a perennial performer, we need to let go of our pride and ego and not let them affect our success.*
- *Our goal should be a life of meaning and purpose, not one inclined to pursuing luxuries.*
- *Through close observation of Marcus Aurelius' meditations, we can distill down three dogmas that can help us in navigating pragmatically in our own experiences without losing our calm. These dogmas are: being content with whatever happens, being just and accepting of others, and being able to apply rules of discernment to our own inner representations of external circumstances. When we live by them, we strengthen our inner fortress and develop the inner attitudes of acceptance to the divine orchestration, justice, serving others, and detachment by being objective.*
- *Epictetus' teachings can be summed up into three core ideas: knowing what we can control and mastering our desires,*

performing our duties and doing the right actions, and learning to think clearly about ourselves, our relationships, and our role within the larger community of humanity.

- *A clear analogy can be observed between ancient Stoic philosophy and modern CBT as there are various concepts and techniques that overlap between the two.*
- *It is a common misconception that Stoicism is an intellectualized philosophical approach that doesn't count emotional responses. In reality, it encourages us to cultivate an attitude of indifference towards things and events that we don't have control over so that we can avoid unnecessary emotional discomfort and pain.*
- *Stoicism not only accommodates emotions but also encourages cultivating a rational love towards humanity and existence as a whole.*
- *Our emotions are our own and we have absolute voluntary control over them.*
- *The concept of antifragility applies to things that benefit from harm caused by volatile and adverse circumstances. Unlike fragile things that break under stress, antifragile things gain an advantage and become better.*
- *We can train both our body and mind to be antifragile.*
- *The quality of an antifragile system is that it not only strengthens you when you face stresses or shockers but also prepares you for any future possible adversities. This happens by the principle of overcompensation, which is the hallmark of antifragility: Strength develops by overcompensating against adversities.*
- *If you want to achieve and maintain extraordinary success in this ever-changing and unpredictable world then antifragility is the most useful skill that you can develop*
- *The Stoics explain that there are different causes of our emotions and some of them include our misaligned beliefs.*

- *Beliefs are patterns that we have cultivated over time and because our emotions are driven by our beliefs, we are responsible for them.*
- *While modern therapies focus on a short-term fix, adopting ancient philosophy is a lifestyle: a life-long discipline to be cultivated and practiced every day.*
- *The Stoics placed huge importance on being in harmony with the Universe and the way it works. They firmly believed in the rational intelligence that permeates everything. Hence, in order to live a happy and peaceful life, they believed it was their duty to act rationally with reason and logic so that they can be better aligned with the Universe.*
- *Plato explained that the foundation of living an extraordinary life is to improve our reasoning consistently and questioning and contemplating the beliefs that we have harbored and accepted.*
- *When we get on the trail of asking deeper questions about life, humanity, meaning, and purpose, we start creating a life that is not only happy and fulfilling but extraordinary in every aspect.*
- *Philosophy can be a wonderful antidote and soothe us whenever we encounter fading humanity.*
- *There are some brilliant takeaways from the ancient Stoic philosophy that can add the depth that we need in our fast-paced lives. The teachings of ethics and relying on practical tools and strategies rather than moral theory are indispensable in today's society.*
- *The movement of reductive materialism or minimalism can be a lifesaver and has parallels with the Stoic philosophy. Decluttering our spaces and our minds can start churning the engines of a meaningful life and bringing more purpose and clarity to us.*
- *The Stoics discouraged getting into unwanted and irrelevant*

emotional trains of thought caused by misunderstandings and inappropriate reactions. Instead, they encouraged cultivating eupatheiai or "good emotional states".

- *We human beings are rational creatures. Our ethical judgments are initiated by 'impressions', which are basically the perceptions that we harbor towards objects around us. Based on our 'assents' to impressions, we form beliefs in our minds. These beliefs dictate how we see the world and our opinions towards things objects and events.*

- *Our success and happiness are much dictated by our internal belief system. In order to live an extraordinary life and fight mediocrity, it is crucial that we first decimate all of our limiting beliefs.*

If you think this book has added value to you and helped you in any way, please consider giving a copy to your loved ones, family members, coworkers, friends or someone you just met, whom you care about and want greater success for. When we help others and give away our time, earnings, and most importantly our heart, the ripple effect ends up bringing more abundance and prosperity to us.

To read more essays on how to create an extraordinary life and become a better version of yourself every day, please visit my website: ParthSawhney.com

References and Suggestions for Further Reading

In addition to the exceptional books mentioned previously in the daily meditations, there are a handful of recent works by some amazing authors and thought leaders that you should most definitely read to develop a Stoic mindset. Here is a comprehensive list of all the best resources on philosophy and the art of living for you:

Aurelius, M., & Hammond, M. (2006). *Meditations (Penguin Classics)*. Penguin Classics.

Aurelius, M., & Hays, G. (2003). *Meditations: A New Translation* (First American PB Edition). Random House Publishing Group.

Aurelius, M., & Waterfield, R. (2021). *Meditations: The Annotated Edition* (Annotated ed.). Basic Books.

Becker, L. C. (2017). *A New Stoicism: Revised Edition* (Rev. ed.). Princeton University Press.

Brennan, T. (2007). *The Stoic Life: Emotions, Duties, and Fate* (1st ed.). Clarendon Press.

E. (1994). *A Manual for Living (Little Book of Wisdom (Harper San Francisco))* (1st ed.). HarperOne.

E., & Dobbin, R. (2008). *Discourses and Selected Writings (Penguin Classics)* (1st ed.). Penguin Classics.

E., & Lebell, S. (2007). *Art of Living: The Classical Manual on Virtue, Happiness, and Effectiveness* (5/27/07 ed.). HarperOne.

E., & Long, G. (2020). *The Enchiridion.* Independently published.

Evans, J. (2013). *Philosophy for Life and Other Dangerous Situations: Ancient Philosophy for Modern Problems* (Illustrated ed.). New World Library.

Goldstein, R. (2015). *Plato at the Googleplex: Why Philosophy Won't Go Away* (Illustrated ed.). Vintage.

Graver, M. (2009). *Stoicism and Emotion* (Illustrated ed.). University of Chicago Press.

Hadot, P., & Chase, M. (2001). *The Inner Citadel: The Meditations of Marcus Aurelius* (Rev. ed.). Harvard University Press.

Holiday, R. (2014). *The Obstacle Is the Way: The Timeless Art of Turning Trials into Triumph* (1st ed.). Portfolio.

Holiday, R. (2016). *Ego Is the Enemy* (1st ed.). Portfolio.

Holiday, R. (2019). *Stillness Is the Key*. Portfolio.

Holiday, R. (2020a). *The Way, the Enemy, and the Key: A Boxed Set of The Obstacle is the Way, Ego is the Enemy & Stillness is the Key*. Portfolio.

Holiday, R. (2020b, August 31). *The Highest Good: An Introduction To The 4 Stoic Virtues*. Daily Stoic. https://dailystoic.com/4-stoic-virtues/

Holiday, R. (2020c, November 28). *Meditations by Marcus Aurelius: Book Summary, Key Lessons and Best Quotes*. Daily Stoic. https://dailystoic.com/meditations-marcus-aurelius/

Holiday, R. (2021a). *Courage Is Calling: Fortune Favors the Brave*. Portfolio.

Holiday, R. (2021b, February 16). *What Is Stoicism? A Definition & 9 Stoic Exercises To Get You Started*. Daily Stoic.

https://dailystoic.com/what-is-stoicism-a-definition-3-stoic-exercises-to-get-you-started/

Holiday, R., & Hanselman, S. (2016). *The Daily Stoic: 366 Meditations on Wisdom, Perseverance, and the Art of Living*. Portfolio.

Holiday, R., & Hanselman, S. (2017). *The Daily Stoic Journal: 366 Days of Writing and Reflection on the Art of Living* (Gjr ed.). Portfolio.

Holiday, R., & Hanselman, S. (2020). *Lives of the Stoics: The Art of Living from Zeno to Marcus Aurelius* (Illustrated ed.). Portfolio.

Holiday, R., & Juhasz, V. (2021). *The Boy Who Would Be King*. Daily Stoic.

Irvine, W. B. (2008). *A Guide to the Good Life: The Ancient Art of Stoic Joy* (1st ed.). Oxford University Press.

Irvine, W. B. (2021). *Stoic Challenge*. Norton.

Pigliucci, M. (2018). *How to Be a Stoic: Using Ancient Philosophy to Live a Modern Life* (Reprint ed.). Basic Books.

Pigliucci, M. (2020). *A Field Guide to a Happy Life: 53 Brief Lessons for Living*. Basic Books.

Pigliucci, M., Cleary, S., & Kaufman, D. (2020). *How to Live a Good Life: A Guide to Choosing Your Personal Philosophy*. Vintage.

Pigliucci, M. G. L. (2021). *Live Like A Stoic: 52 Exercises for Cultivating a Good Life*. Rider.

Pigliucci, M., & Lopez, G. (2019). *A Handbook for New Stoics: How to Thrive in a World Out of Your Control—52 Week-by-Week Lessons* (Illustrated ed.). The Experiment.

Robertson, D. (2018). *Stoicism and the Art of Happiness: Practical Wisdom for Everyday Life (Teach Yourself)* (2nd ed.). Teach Yourself.

Robertson, D. (2019). *The Philosophy of Cognitive-Behavioural Therapy (CBT): Stoic Philosophy as Rational and Cognitive Psy-*

chotherapy (2nd ed.). Routledge.

Robertson, D. (2020). *How to Think Like a Roman Emperor.* Griffin.

Rufus, M., Lutz, C. E., & Reydams-Schils, G. (2020). *That One Should Disdain Hardships: The Teachings of a Roman Stoic.* Yale University Press.

S., & Costa, C. D. N. (2005). *On the Shortness of Life: Life Is Long if You Know How to Use It (Penguin Great Ideas)* (1st ed.). Penguin Books.

Salzgeber, J., & Salzgeber, N. (2019). *The Little Book of Stoicism: Timeless Wisdom to Gain Resilience, Confidence, and Calmness* (Illustrated ed.). Jonas Salzgeber.

Sawhney, P. (2020). *The Daily Apple: 366 Meditations on Growth, Persistence, and the Art of Exceptional Living* (Vol. 1). Parth Sawhney.

Seneca, L. A., & Campbell, R. (1969). *Letters from a Stoic (Penguin Classics)* (Reprint ed.). Penguin Books.

Sherman, N. (2007). *Stoic Warriors: The Ancient Philosophy behind the Military Mind* (Illustrated ed.). Oxford University Press.

Stockdale, J. B. (1993). *Courage Under Fire: Testing Epictetus's Doctrines in a Laboratory of Human Behavior (Hoover Essays)* (1st ed.). Hoover Institution Press.

Taleb, N. N. (2012). *Antifragile: Things That Gain from Disorder (Incerto)* (First Edition). Random House.

Parth Sawhney is an author and success mentor to high-achievers all around the world. Through his writing and other meaningful creations, Parth shares life-changing ideas, insights, and resources related to personal development, philosophy, success mindset, and the human condition. His recent books include *The Daily Apple, Thriving in the New Normal, The Way of the Karma Yogi,* and *The Detachment Manifesto.* When he is not working, Parth enjoys spending time in coffee shops and taking long walks.